Contents

Some words are shown in bold, **like this.** Find out what they mean in the glossary on page 23.

What is shyness?

jealous

angry

happy

proud

sad

Shyness is a **feeling.** It is normal to have many kinds of feelings every day.

Dealing with Feeling...
Shy

Isabel Thomas

Illustrated by Clare Elsom

Raintree is an imprint of Capstone Global Library Limited, a company incorporated in England and Wales having its registered office at 7 Pilgrim Street, London, EC4V 6LB – Registered company number: 6695582

www.raintreepublishers.co.uk
myorders@raintreepublishers.co.uk

Text © Capstone Global Library Limited 2013
First published in hardback in 2013
Paperback edition first published in 2014
The moral rights of the proprietor have been asserted.

Edited by Dan Nunn, Rebecca Rissman, and Catherine Veitch
Designed by Philippa Jenkins
Original illustrations © Clare Elsom
Illustrated by Clare Elsom
Production by Victoria Fitzgerald
Originated by Capstone Global Library Ltd
Printed and bound in China

ISBN 978 1 406 25044 2 (hardback)
16 15 14 13 12
10 9 8 7 6 5 4 3 2 1

ISBN 978 1 406 25054 1 (paperback)
17 16 15 14
10 9 8 7 6 5 4 3 2 1

British Library Cataloguing in Publication Data
Thomas, Isabel.
Shy. -- (Dealing with Feeling...)
155.2'32-dc23
A full catalogue record for this book is available from the British Library.

Some feelings are not nice to have. Shyness is not a nice feeling. We might feel shy when we try new things or speak in front of people.

How do we know when someone is feeling shy?

Our faces and bodies can show other people how we are feeling. Some people may speak quietly when they are feeling shy.

Other people may not speak at all. Sometimes a person might look unfriendly, when really they are just feeling shy.

What does it feel like to be shy?

Shyness can make us feel a bit scared around other people. We might worry about doing something **embarrassing.**

Shyness can mean we do not say or do the things we would like to. Not joining in can make us feel bad about ourselves.

Is it normal to feel shy?

Sometimes we might feel shy for a short time. It is normal to feel shy when you do something for the first time.

Take time to get used to a new **activity.** Watch other people and see how they act. This will help you to feel more **confident.**

How can I deal with shyness?

Many people feel shy when they
meet new people for the first time.
You might feel like you do not
know what to say.

The best thing to do when you feel shy is to smile. A shy face may look scared or grumpy. A smiling face always looks friendly.

How do I start talking to new people?

A big change, such as starting a new school, can be scary. You might feel shy because you do not know what the children and teachers will be like.

A good way to make new friends is to ask people questions about themselves. Maybe you like the same books or computer games!

How can I get better at talking in front of people?

Many people feel **nervous** when they have to speak in front of lots of people. This might make you too shy to put up your hand in class.

Practise reading aloud to your family or friends. The more you practise speaking to a group, the easier it will get.

What if I feel shy all the time?

Sometimes shy **feelings** can be very strong and stop us from doing things we enjoy. You might feel shy if how you look or the things you do make you different from other people.

The best way to deal with shy feelings is to talk about them. Share your worries with someone. They might tell you what they do to feel less shy.

How can I help someone who is feeling shy?

Everyone feels shy sometimes. Ask your friends, teachers, or parents what makes them feel shy.

Next time you spot someone who is not joining in, remember that they might be feeling shy. Help them to make friends by being friendly yourself.

Make a shyness toolbox

Write down some tips to help you deal with shy **feelings.**

Practise doing new things with your friends or family.

Relax and take deep breaths to keep your body calm.

Give yourself a treat every time you try something new.

Give someone a **compliment.** This is a good way to start talking to someone new.

Talk about your feelings with someone you trust.

Don't be afraid to ask for help. Everyone needs help sometimes.

Ask people questions about themselves.

Smile – a smiling face always looks friendly!

Glossary

activity something you do for fun

compliment say something nice about someone

confident feeling that you can do something well

embarrassing something that makes you feel awkward, as if you have done something wrong

feeling something that happens inside our minds. It can affect our bodies and the way we behave.

nervous scared or worried about doing something

Find out more

Books

All Kinds of Feelings: A Lift-the-Flap Book, Emma Brownjohn (Tango Books, 2003)

Poindexter Makes a Friend, Mike Twohy (Simon & Schuster, 2011)

Websites

bbc.co.uk/scotland/education/health/feelings

kidshealth.org/kid/feeling

pbskids.org/arthur/games/aboutface

Index